SEX and the
RECESSION

SEX and the
RECESSION

How to afford sex in the Recession

by
Copstick and Maclean

with illustrations by
Michael Faraday

SEX and THE RECESSION

Erotic Review Books
London 2009

Special thanks to:
Nichi Hodgson
Andrea Gherkin
Shirley Balls
The Right Rev. Rory McRoary
Professor Claus Schnurr

ERB, 31 Sinclair Road,
LONDON W14 0NS
Tel: +44 (0) 207 371 1532
Email: enquiries@eroticprints.org
Web: www.eroticprints.org
© 2009 MacHo Ltd, London UK

Illustrations by Michael Faraday

ISBN: 978-1-904989-60-8

Printed and bound in Spain by Litografia Rosés. Barcelona

ABOUT THE AUTHORS

Kate COPSTICK is blah, blah, blah and so on and so forth, more of the same, just tell it like it is, leave the reader in absolutely no doubt as to all there is to know about this brilliant authoress, superstar, superbiker and total Goddess.

Jamie MACLEAN is editor of the *Erotic Review* and is willing to take on any other jobs he can find in these hard times. These include freelance journalism, book editing and publishing, escort work and wife-sitting.

CONTENTS

CONTENTS

What do a Braun electric toothbrush and Internet dating agencies have in common? Both are in their own curious way illustrations of the Recession. The toothbrush can double thriftily as a vibrator and, for some reason, as yet unclear, an increasingly large number of people are turning to online dating. In *Sex and the Recession*, we'll try to dispell that sense of gloom, and get you on the right track for some superior Recession Sex. Don't expect this book to be an instant panacea for these troubled economic times. But thinking positively about sex sure as hell beats worrying about money.

Only trouble is, there's a definite link between money and sex. It's silly to think that sexual passion will somehow transmute poverty into a golden experience. It won't. Infatuation doesn't last forever. Look at any successful contract between a whore and her client or a wife and her husband: they both rely on the client/spouse being able to come up with hard cash on a regular basis. In the longterm, there's no such thing as a free fuck.

We dedicate this book to the poor, the nouveau-poor and those who have lost, or are about to lose, their jobs. Or even those who were unlucky enough to invest all their cash with Madoff and are down to their last few million. It's all relative. The pain's the same.

On the other hand, the Recession is quite good news for those in secure employment. There are bargains galore, your money goes further and you can enjoy the warm glow of charitable fulfilment as you drop 10p into the hat of the ex-Lehman Bros employee panhandling at the bottom of your street. But for the rest of us it's more a case of teetering on the edge of negative equity, repossession or even the novel experience of unemployment benefit or bankruptcy.

Never mind. It will all be over sooner than you think. And even though it may be a temporarily painful experience, no one's saying it has to be a puritanical one. Unless you actually derive physical pleasure from such an act, there's no need to beat yourself up over this. God isn't punishing you for the follies of the bankers.

So enjoy life and fornicate for all you're worth. It's life-enhancing, life-affirming and we'll show you in the following pages, often eminently affordable. Even in a Recession.

PART ONE

Single Sex

Chapter One: Masturbation

"Don't knock masturbation. It's sex with someone I love", said Woody Allan to Diane Keaton.

Better than that, it is sex with someone guaranteed to know exactly what you want: where, how, how hard, how soft.

Few things can stave off a decent orgasm off for a girl quite like having to mutter instructions which always seem to end up sounding like the closing stages of an airplane disaster movie "Keep the nose up... *up!* Yes now lower the flaps...".

And I know there is no cock as frustrated as a cock in the wrong hands... or as painful as a cock in the wrong mouth.

So, chaps, embrace the Recession and the lack of financial wherewithal to wine and dine and romance your genital stimulatress of choice and stimulate yourself.

And ladies, kick off those high high shoes worn to elongate the leg, thrust out the breasts, round the buttocks and hurt, hurt; leave those sexy little outfits that cost a fortune and fit like a tourniquet in the closet; ignore everything that L'Oreal can do for you because 'you're worth it!' (ask yourself, as you gaze at a 'Hot Auburn' bank statement, ladies, are *they*?) and relax and let yourself go with the one person for whom you never have to fake it.

'If you don't love yourself, you cannot love others,' said the Dalai Lama and, although not widely acknowledged as a sexpert, the old veggie was right.

So learn to love yourself… treat yourself to little treats that only you know you like… call yourself up and leave messages for yourself whispering the words you know will turn you on… put on your favourite porno for yourself and know that you won't mind you watching it while you build up an orgasm… perfume the room with your favourite scented candles and relax knowing that you won't complain about the 'pong'.

Then find your favourite position… you know you'll like it… disappear into your favourite fantasy secure in the knowledge that you won't mind if you call someone else's name out in the throes of passion... and treat yourself just as you know you like to be treated afterwards.

'The best things in life are free,' said someone else. Possibly a confirmed masturbator in a recession. Try it. I think you'll find at least one of them is.

Do look into buying a camcorder and setting yourself up as online titillation. www.FlicktheBeanwithFelicity.com or www.StrokeAlongaSimon.com could be a lovely little earner in these financially difficult times.

Do consider setting up video conference calling – and be reassured that you won't lose touch with friends and family just because none of you can afford to go out any more but have all been smart enough to buy this book and try the handy hints in Chapter One.

Do invest in a few cheap full length mirrors. You won't feel so alone and there is something incredibly sexy about staring deep into your own eyes as you cum.

"The reason I love Jim," wrote Suzy Hickford about the legendary Jim Haynes, *"is that he comes while he masturbates me and I don't even have to touch him. And then afterwards he says it was like his third ever orgasm when he was about thirteen."*

Don't even think about buying a camcorder and setting yourself up as online titillation. Your finances will (with a following wind and a change of government) recover. Your reputation never would.

Don't ever set up video conference calls. 'Keeping in touch' is not meant to be taken literally. Friends and family will bar your calls and change their numbers. Then, when you can afford it again, you will have no one to go out and enjoy yourself with.

Don't have mirrors anywhere near you. Not unless you are one of the few people who live up to their own fantasies. If you are, you are an egomaniacal narcissist and undoubtedly have mirrors everywhere anyway.

If not, it will all end in tears as you see

your wobbliest parts from three different angles and are forced to seek (very expensive) therapy for problems with self loathing and low self esteem.

Now pay close attention, we only have a few pages to explain this (this is Sex in the RECESSION, ergo you can't afford to pay much for the book, so we can only afford to print 128 pages) and it is quite complicated.

The Recession affects us all, but like alcohol, Marmite and Country Music, it affects us all in different ways.

Luckily, for the single sex-seeker who is already fully aquainted with what we will call here The Sexual Economy, it is possible to minimise the horizontal damage the Recession will do to your sex life.

Of course, the male sex life is much more fragile and vulnerable to an economic downturn than the female. Because men, almost universally, are the ones who have to pay what is colloquially known as the Cervix Charge – anything from an evening of compliments and attention, through dinner and drinks, to marriage and children.

The female merely has to work out what sort

of price she can command and market herself accordingly. Now don't raise those expensively threaded eyebrows, ladies. You know you do it. Well, OK. Maybe subconsciously.

"The first thing on earth to be sold was cunt," said Germaine Greer once. "It's the paradigm of all selling. I don't know if we've a hope in hell of overturning that. But I'm determined to try".

Luckily she has failed.

The old HPP (Horizontal Payment Plan) continues to buy a girl those little extra luxuries. Even though you might not want to admit it.

And that is not going to change.

All the Recession has done is to alter the Exchange Rate.

To throw a financial spanner in the working of that hairy chequebook.

But fear not, this chapter will equip you with all you need to know to get the most out of what you have got... no matter how little the Recession has left you with. For ease of explanation, please turn to the page opposite

ONE F	Visual Viagra Physical Perfection	ONE M
TWO F	Pretty Gorgeous	TWO M
THREE F	Brushes Up Well	THREE M
FOUR F	Primark Sale Day 2	FOUR M
FIVE F	Uglies	FIVE M

Believe it or not there are some times when honesty is absolutely necessary when trying to get yourself laid. Primarily – in fact almost exclusively – that is when assessing your likelihood of bagging the object of your desire. And, don't worry, you are only required to be honest with yourself. Failure so to do will inevitably result in one of two things; tragic underachievement or deep, deep disappointment and humiliation.

So look into the mirror, people, and prepare to admit what you are.

Then acknowledge that people generally get their leg over someone else on the same level. Males will fuck down the scale if it means the difference between getting laid or not getting laid (see infra). Females are much more complicated, (see infra).

ONES

You are a One if you are physically flawless. Your teeth are visible in a power cut, your skin is like silk, your hands are soft and your buttocks like two hard-boiled eggs in a sling. You are a member of the nubility *.

The **Female One** has the face of an angel, the eyes of a devil, long, slim legs and a pair of Hush Puppies* that stop traffic. She is in every possible physical way absolutely perfect. The scale is brutally superficial and so, unfair as it frequently seems to females further down the scale, the FAFCAM* and the FAFTAS* female will tend to be classed as a One. These are the faces and forms that gather interest in wank-banks* everywhere

The **Male One** has a jaw that could slice prosciutto, abs like a cobbled street, a glorious

---

Nubility: a small class of physically perfect beings that give a rush of ' blue blood' to anyone in their vicinity

Hush Puppies: breasts of such magnitude and pulchritude that the sight of them renders men utterly speechless

FAFCAM: Fit as Fuck, Common As Muck

FAFTAS: Fit As Fuck, Thick As Shit

Wank-bank: the collection of images in the mind which are withdrawn and used when a chap decides to Bank with Barclays head of hair that speaks of testosterone in abundance and the kind of jewellery showcase* that would make Tiffany herself weep hot salt tears of desire and which opens to reveal Pink Steel* of the finest quality. Again, due to the calibration of the scale, the TartThrob* will frequently (although arguably erroneously) be referred to as a One.

Ones have sex with Ones. Why would they want to (other than as detailed infra) 'fuck down' and how could any lesser being (other than as detailed infra) 'fuck up'? There is no negotiation. Don't even think about going there.

Why would Angelina Jolie fuck you when she can fuck Brad Pitt? And vice versa.

And in the Recession? Even the female One can, amazingly enough, find herself in a vulnerable situation in the Recession. She is

*Jewellery Showcase: male genitalia, frequently as displayed in tight fitting underpants (see Armani/Beckham ad)
*Pink Steel: an almost unfeasibly hard erection. Also referred to as a Diamond Cutter.
*TartThrob: a low-grade 'hunk' type who has unaccountable sexual appeal to the less discriminating female eg the young David Hasselhoff, Peter Andre

HMP* – incredibly demanding and on the maintainance scale, just below a F1 Ferrari.

In a Recession, her price might just be too high, even for a male One.

Which is not at all a bad thing for the female Two, Three, Four or even Five.

The male One will, if unable or unwilling to meet the demands of the female One, look elsewhere. If it comes to a downward fuck or no fuck, he'll go for the downward fuck (see Deal Or No Deal below) and the rest of the scale of womankind is after his beautiful bone like Mother Hubbard's Dog. Those males who have achieved One-ness through power, fame or money – could, when the Recession takes that away, suffer relegation right back to their natural rating.

The heterosexual female One will never willingly, consciously fuck anything but a male One. Or Pseudo-One. Thanks to the complex nature of female sexuality, even a male Five can elevate himself to attract even female Ones by using any combination of three simple accessories: money, fame and power.

The more you have of all or any of these, the less the female will care about your physical shortcomings, qv Henry Kissinger, Hugh Hefner, Ricky Gervais. These individuals are known as Pseudo-Ones.

*HMP: High Maintainance Pussy

TWOS

If you are a Two you are very attractive. You will always turn heads although you don't necessarily dislocate necks.

In many places, where the totty pool is not particularly extensive, the Two will be able to pass as a One – much of Central Belt Scotland, The Midlands and Croyden for example.

The **Female Two** will have the complete package – top to toe – and look as good with her clothes on the floor as on her body. For a Two ranking, there should be a reasonable lack of artifice otherwise Two becomes Three. Breasts should be at least a SBH*, collars and cuffs should match the hair.

The **Male Two** will be aquainted with the basics of grooming. Body hair is, of course acceptable, but should be managed. Back hair, for example, can drop a Two to a Four.

And in the Recession? Female Twos do have a tendancy to imagine that they are Ones and act accordingly (see also above). This will get them absolutely nowhere in the Recession, unless they can target a One male who can no longer afford a One female. Two males will go for another Two with less attitude – let's face it, they have enough on their minds with their finances in a fankle.

Low-grade Twos might even find themselves dropping down to a Three rating if they find themselves unable to maintain the look.

Male Twos who have achieved Two-ness through the money/fame/power thing will face relegation, but this is the category which includes many professional stand up comics. The female insistence that 'someone who makes me laugh' is a top priority in a mate will elevate a male to a Two, although almost never to a One. And comics usually thrive in hard times as a) it gives them material and b) they are usually embittered, depressive types anyway an feel at home in hard times. Other males from the lower ratings could try brushing up their humourous small talk. It's free and it works.

*SBH: Standard British Handful

THREES

The Three is a many and varied thing, and can alter in appearance from one occasion to the next.

Female Threes can be less than a Two and more than a Four for a variety of reasons: many MILFs* and GILFs* are Threes, as are BOBFOCs* and their opposite, FFTBBBs*. Aside from them, the kind of female who is never seen without full make-up, spends more on her hair than she does on her holiday and would spread manure on her face if a beauty expert told her it would 'diminish the appearance of lines and wrinkles' tends to be a Three. The female Three is incapable of doing anything without a minimum of three hours preparation, will cover your bedlinen in Max Factor and probably wake you at 5am when she arises to make a start on face and hair for the day. Breast men should be aware that female Threes have a tendancy to sport Millenium Domes*.

Female Threes want to bag themselves a male One or Two. They will play hard to get with fellow Threes and are more or less off limits to Fours and Fives (unless the old money/fame/ power/ big car is brought into play)

The **Male Three** is also a creature of many parts, some of which let down the rest: moobs, beer bellies and having teeth like a crossword puzzle are frequent problems. A male Two can drop to a Three when, on closer inspection, he turns out to be hung like a hummingbird and a complete stranger to personal hygiene.

Male Threes will, of course, fantasise about female Ones and Twos but be happy with a Three or a Four.

And in the Recession? Female Threes are very vulnerable as the cost of keeping a female a Three and not a Two is considerable. It costs a Three as much to be a Three as it does a One to maintain One-ness. But, to much less impressive effect. So female Threes may find themselves slipping in the ratings.

Any males thinking of reducing the costs of sex with a Three by buying in bulk (i.e. cohabiting) should remember that two bathrooms are absolutely necessary or he may never get in to drop the kids off at the pool in his own home again.

Such a male should consider finding a top end Two until the Recession is over.

* MILF: Mummy I'd Like to Fuck
*GILF: Granny I'd Like to Fuck aka Punani Granny
*BOBFOC: Body Off Baywatch, Face Off Crimewatch – a lady with a fabulous body and a face like she's been jogging behind a gritter
*FBTBBB: Face By Titian, Body By Bosch: a lady with a beautiful face and a body like a medieval vision of hell.
*Millenium Domes: The contents of an uplift, underwired bra. Very impressive when viewed from outside but when you get in there is bugger all of interest to see.

FOURS

As described in the diagram, Primark Sale Day Two – OK, but possibly slightly soiled, distressed, been handled a lot and obviously not impressive enough to be picked up by those who got first choice.

This is a large group. Let's be honest. It catches most of those who fall from higher categories for a variety of reasons. OK. Mainly age. Contrary to what they bleat, age *does* wither her.

Female Fours include the GMPG*, because their ability, when seen from afar, to appear much more attractive than they are close up means that their ability to attract is much higher than the Five they would otherwise be.

Female Fours, of course, will always set their sights on at least a Two. And, in the Recession might just get one (see 'Deal or No Deal', etc., under 'Fives' below).

Male Fours could try brushing themselves up to a Three if they can, or pick up some fallen female Threes who can't afford the plaster and paint to keep themselves up there. Male and female Fours should consider going down the money/fame route. It isn't even necessary to any ability for anything to gain at least one of them, as the ongoing plague of Reality TV shows can turn you from ignorant, unpleasant, ugly waste of sperm to national celebrity overnight... and in a bizarre unfairness, the stories of any resulting sexual conquests will be snapped up by the tabloids resulting in more money and more fame resulting in more sexual conquests etc., etc.. Just a pity that the Recession doesn't seem to be hitting the budgets for these fucking shows.

*GPMG: named after the army's General Purpose Machine Gun which is regarded as "good at range but unbelievably messy close up".

FIVES

Fives are, to be brutally honest, simply BFU*. Other than to those with what we will call 'niche' tastes.

Fives, however, frequently offer what is known as 'loose chips in the bag'* and so not to be dismissed out of hand.

Female Fives

These are times of mixed fortune for the female Five.

Normally, thanks to the eventually indiscriminating sexual nature of the male, even a female Five has a reasonable chance of finding something attractive wiping his feet on her welcome mat.

Given the complex system of tests, demands, financial/professional/ personal qualifications generally required by the female One, Two,

---

*BFU: Butt Fuck Ugly. When a man or a woman is grossly physically unattractive. Oh dear, our American cousins are so uncompromisingly expressive at times...

*Loose Chips in the Bag: a reference to the McDonalds bag where there is sometimes a happy discovery of some extra loose chips at the bottom. In this context, the 'loose chips' can be the ability to deep throat, a father who runs a pub, a cock like a toddler's arm holding a grapefruit, etc..

Three and Four, it is not unknown, even in non-Recessionary times, for a female Five to make the beast with two backs with a male Four, Three, Two or even One. Now the Recession has us in its grip, the opportunities for Fives are on the up, as the higher ranked females price themselves out of the market.

It is more or less accepted as fact that Fives try harder and are more grateful.

Which is attractive. Also, the female Five learns, early on, the Power of Easy. Which is *very* attractive.

Even the Frombie* or the Wheelie Bint* knows that there is a Happy Hunting Ground created for them by the irritating games-playing of, to differing degrees, almost all other women.

We have only to look at time-honoured, male-biased mating rituals such as:

Deal or No Deal*, Stick at 15* or Go Ugly Early* to appreciate the sexual opportunities open to the female, as long as she can achieve some sort of objectivity.

*Deal or No Deal: This is when someone (usually male), in a club or bar has managed to attract a potential bed-partner, albeit probably no more than a FOUR, possibly a FIVE. He or she then has to decide whether to take what they have or hold out for something better and run the risk of going home alone, in the manner of Noel Edmunds groin-dessicatingly banal but inexplicably popular TV game show

This is also known as ***'Sticking at Fifteen'** (from the game of Blackjack where the aim is to get cards whose values add up to twenty one) where someone settles for a low score because they are unwilling to risk losing everything.

It is also known as ***'Going Ugly Early'**

*Frombie: a young lady so utterly lacking in physical appeal that the only way to have sex with her is 'from behind'

*Wheelie Bint: A young lady so lacking in charms that, at most, she only gets taken out once a week

Male Fives

Even in normal times, the Five male has huge problems in getting laid. A female is unlikely to go all the way to Cockfosters for a Five unless he does something radical. Blackmail and Rohypnol are effective but carry the danger of doing prison time which would further diminish the Five's ranking. Finding a girl with pathological self-esteem issues or who is blind is an option. And, given the right target, begging and weeping has been known to work.

Sense of humour will, it is rumoured, take a Five to at least a Three, possibly a Two. Elevation can also be achieved through by having money, power and/or fame (see Ones).

However, this does not always work

The Hummersexual is a man so devoid of attractiveness, and so lacking in the trouser department that he only has a chance of getting laid by getting behind the wheel of the biggest, most ridiculously oversized and overpriced passenger vehicle money can buy. He is never likely to get above a Three.

Sadly, now we have The Recession, the money option has deserted many and with it the power and the fame. Or indeed any permutation of the foregoing.

So male Fives are more trapped in the sexual ghetto of their own unattractiveness than ever.

But even for you chaps, in the deepest depths of Recessions financial and sexual, there is hope!

There is a North Sumatran court record of one Mr Masib Nasution being asked to explain the fact that he had married 121 times and made a huge fortune from dowries. "I was an ugly child," he said, "and as I grew older the ugliness increased. By the time I was 30 people considered me to be hideous. Then I met a woman who advised me to take up smoking and, when I was about to propose, just blow the smoke in my beloved's eyes. I followed the advice and that is why I am here today."

HANDY HINT: of course the 'any port in a storm' effect will come into play during a Recession, but for a bit of a 'wildcard' experience, a Three, Four or even a Five of either sex could score by offering someone higher up the scale a tantalising Roy Walker Moment*. In stressful times like these, the idea of doing something just a bit 'bad' can be hugely attractive.

*Roy Walker Moment: so called after the catchphrase of the genial Irish Catchphrase host "it's good but it's not right". So: shagging your best friend's mum/sister/brother/father, your teacher, your partner's mother/sister/brother/father etc.

PART TWO

Partnered Sex

Chapter Three: Partnered Sex for Him the Girlfriend

After masturbation, partnered sex is by far the cheapest, unless determinedly procreative. Then it becomes the most expensive. Children, especially those of aspirational couples, act as a sexual disincentive. Daddy's far too exhausted by working extra long hours in order to keep his job and so be able to pay Arabella's extortionate boarding school fees and Mummy's far more obsessed by toddler Tarquin's sleepover (and getting a good night's sleep herself) than having erotic high jinks in any shape, form or meaningful quantity. Parenthood − curiously its natural enemy − pays only lip service to good sex.

If disaster strikes and negative equity forces you into bankruptcy and you lose your over-mortgaged home to the bank, try to look on the bright side. Couples often bond ever more strongly in the face of adversity. On the other hand, when the going gets tough is frequently when the tough get going. And boys, if you don't already know this, be warned: the female of the species is much tougher than the male.

Do sell your 48-inch plasma screen television. Thus you may have just enough energy to enjoy some desultory sex before falling into a deep, anxiety-ridden slumber. Coming a close second after Tarquin and Arabella, addictive celebrity-reality TV and/or old *Terminator* movies are both industrial-strength libido suppressors.

Do put your children up for adoption on e-bay and see what they'll fetch. I'm not sure if this is legal, but it's worth a try. Why? See above.

Do sell up and become a member of the rural set. Once you've got rid of the rugrats and the TV, is there any point in staying in the city? Some would argue yes, look at all the culture. Culture? Hah! Get real. You won't be able to afford it. Anyway, in the country you'll be able to catch up on your reading. Alright, alright, we know the *real* reason you're joining the ruralists is because you've been dying to try it with a nice, placid, Aberdeen Angus cow called Heather.

Don't become a member of the rural set. It's

downhill all the way once you don the green wellies. Inbreeding, bestiality, milkmaids and gamekeepers.

Don't start having an affair. Boys will simply not be able to afford this. Girls will find the transgressive nature of extramarital sex quite exhilarating to begin with, then depressing, when they realise that the net worth of the male they're having an affair with might just be even lower than their husband's.

Don't become so obsessive about having/ not having sex that it gets on your partner's tits. You can't afford a divorce, either.

Don't start eating large amounts of comfort food to compensate for the shitty time you're having or you'll end up being too fat for your partner to fancy you just as the Recession ends. Treat it as a slimming oportunity.

PART THREE

Fetish Sex

Once considered perversion, there is no more Recession-friendly sexual persuasion (other than celibacy, but we are rather assuming if you are using your crunched credit to pay for this book then you are in the market for a little added-value mattress dancing) than true fetishism.

True fetishism replaces a 'normal' sexual partner with a) a piece of that partner: the foot, the buttock, the breast, b) an item of clothing: knickers, bra, or c) another inanimate object: a lamp, a knife, a cup. DO you see where we are going here? Even in a Recession, if you can work up a bit of a passion for a housebrick, or manage to get all of a quiver over an ashtray, then you are going to become the envy of your friends as, time after time, you slump in a glorious post-coital haze onto the sofa, clutching a packet of digestives.

Some of you – those with a penchant for shagging footballers, girlbands or soap actors - will not even notice the lack of stimulating conversation or witty banter.

If you can achieve a good-going, orgasm-inducing fetish you will have eliminated, with one stroke (well… obviously more than just one stroke) all those things that can stand in the way of a truly Jolly Roger. Just hold back from introducing your sink plunger to your parents and friends. They might not understand.

Some say that there can be no compromise when it comes to fetish equipment – that its very excellence or luxury is integral and crucial to the experience. We can't argue with them and we hope they have stockpiled a good supply to tide them over the Recesssion. Others may not have been so lucky, and so games such as the Castaway Fantasy might rather suit them.

The Castaway Fantasy: you have been shipwrecked and washed up on what looks to be a desert island. You wake up to find that you are stark naked and your clothes and underwear appear to have been lost in the process, but among the flotsam and jetsam washed up along the shore you find enough to more or less adequately cover your rude bits. Just as you finish doing this, a handsome/pretty Man/Woman Friday pops out from behind a palm tree and...

Of course what you, the innocent shipwrecked, does *not* know is that Man/Woman F. has carefully laid out what he or she wants you to wear in line with what their own fetish is. So don't act surprised if you see a black binliner, two coconut shells, 500 grammes of Lurpak, some string, a carefully shredded issue of yesterday's *Financial Times* and a hand-crafted butt-plug with streamers stuck to one end. Instinctively, you'll know just what to do with them.

Which brings us to the part where we should probably tell you how to fashion an enema kit out of an old hot water bottle, a length of rubber tubing, some of those thick red Royal Mail rubber bands and the right sort of glue.

We're sorry, but life's too short. You really have to work this sort of thing out for yourselves – it's all part of the fun. In any case remember that Necessity is the Mother of

Invention and we have no idea of what your filthy needs might be. But a word of caution: if you live in a small community, best go to a large DIY supermarket and not the local village chemist or hardware shop for some of your more exotic purchases. Ordering thirty square metres of rubber sheeting might earn you some curious glances on the high street.

Don't use mains power when creating a homemade sex toy. The orgasm you enjoy will be unlike any other, but it might also be your last.

Do think about giving watersports a go if you've never tried it. True, it's not everyone's *tasse de thé*, but you have to admit, it's the ultimate in recycling and completely free.

Professor Claus Schnurr says: In my time with the Yumungi tribe I often came across some extraordinary examples of fetish and ritual extemporisation. On one occasion when the tribal elders couldn't remember the point of the ritual or, indeed, how it went, they simply attempted to have sex with each other while everyone else watched. It lasted nearly four hours - a deeply moving experience.

Shirley Balls says: My gorgeous young man Kent (I call him Superman, of course!!) and I get up to all sorts of naughty things together. Too many to go into here, but my fave is when I sit on his face while watching TV and we pretend he's a chair. Wicked!!

PART FOUR

Sex With More Than Two People

Chapter Five: Swinging

Sad to relate, the old saying, 'there's safety in numbers', doesn't really apply when it comes to sex. It would be comforting to think that, as you set off for the Browns' (no, not *those* Browns) key-chucking, spouse-swapping party, that warm feeling of belonging to a club, a band of brothers and sisters, of being part of the gang, will wash over you. It's more likely that you'll be a bag of nervous jitters. As a sexual recreation, swinging is a landscape strewn with emotional mines and burnt-out marriages, and populated by the predatory or insecure of either sex.

Of course, there are swinging parties where everyone knows what they're doing, are happy to be there and they often have a memorable time. But this tends to be the exception rather than the rule. If you're curious, try it, but don't expect too much. Both of you subscribing to a speed dating (see Part Five) event might be a safer, saner bet. The idea behind swinging, however is 'what's good for the goose is good for the gander'. In other words, 'if you're going to screw around, then so am I'. It's not so much a case of 'Those Browns know an awfully nice group of people and we would really rather like to join their set', more 'If I'm going to screw around, then I'd feel much better if she was, too, because then she won't be able to snipe at me from the moral high ground.'

Do wear clean underwear

Don't get too drunk because you're nervous or you'll fail to perform well and get asked back again.

Chapter Six: Orgies

Like Swinging, orgies are for more than two people. A lot more. They've been going on since the time of the ancient Greeks, and quite possibly before that. But in this country our orgiastic traditions are at least venerable, though not quite so ancient. From the Middle Ages, we have been behaving badly in this way. Bullenger, in his *The Christian State of Matrimonye*, describes the celebrations after a peasant wedding thus:

> *'Then there is such a renninge, leapinge and flynginge amongst them, then there is such a lyftinge up and discouering of damesels clothes and of other wemens apparell that a man might think all these dauncers had cast all shame behinde them and were become starke madde and out of their wittes.'*

So not much change there, then. But my point is, orgies, like weddings, are expensive to lay on. You've got to organise a marquee, in case it rains. Champagne should flow like water and you should probably get one of those catering companies to set it all up, hand those very pricey little canapes around and present you with a massive bill at the end.

It's not surprising that our cunning mediaeval ancestors waited for a wedding to come along, knowing that they could combine it with an all-out sexual free-for-all, no holes barred, plus lots of food and drink.

If they could afford it then, surely you can afford it now. So when the Ponsonby-Smythes marry off their Lucinda to that frightfully nice young man, slyly suggest you pay for half of it and that you'll be inviting 'just a few pals'. Then advertise it on www.Craigslist. com and sell tickets for £50 per couple. You'll probably make a small profit. On the other hand, Lucinda Ponsonby-Smythe will never forgive you.

Do go dressed as Emperor Caligula or an incestuous Borgia Pope.

Don't wear *any* underwear.

PART FIVE

A Recessional Alphabet

Anal Sex

If she's feeling sexually adventurous and suggests trying 'the other place' (and yes, this *is* a somewhat coy reference to her rectum via her lubricated anal sphincter) then why not go for it? Around 40% of women take it up the bum with varying degrees of pleasure or pain, or both. And if *he's* feeling sexually adventurous (very), he might get over his irrational homophobic fears and agree to you donning your strap-on and giving him one up the Elephant & Castle.

And in the Recession? Limited, but one of the cheapest forms of contraception, bar abstinence.

Aphrodisiac

Used to be reading your bank statement every month or fingering those first class tickets to the Seychelles. Now it's 25mg of Viagra, if you're lucky. The canny Scots know a thing or two about bargain basement aphrodisiacs.

And in the Recession? In the land of Connery and McGregor, a can of Special Brew is known as a 'Leg Opener'.

Adultery

Just in case you've led a *very* sheltered life, this is when a wife or husband has a sexual relationship with a third party, secretly or against their spouse's wishes. Our grasp on religiously-inspired law is tenuous, but in certain far-off lands, we hear that adultery is punishable by stoning to death. If you're a woman, that is. If you're a man, you get admiring glances from your buddies and told not to do it again – for at least a year. But we digress.

And in the Recession? You can't even think of being able to afford the sort of reconciliation gifts that might or might not persuade your spouse to forgive you, let alone a divorce. So don't get caught.

Prof Schnurr says: Absolutely! Don't get caught. I remember back in 1967 when my ex-wife, Frau Professor Elfriede Schnurr, found me in flagrante with my Japanese research assistant Yuki who was introducing me to the delights of naked sashimi. There was hell to pay.

Shirley Balls says: Don't get caught. Unless you think he/she is up for making it a threesome. Phwoarrrr! Way to go, tiger/tigress!!!

IS FOR

Bestiality

Fur- and feather-fucking. From household petting to farmyard frolics, this comes under the cheap date section. Unless of course you get caught and there are legal fees and vetinary bills involved.

And in the Recession? You might want to consider a cheap flight to Belgium, Denmark, Finland, Germany, Hungary, Mexico, the Netherlands, Norway, Sweden, or Switzerland. In Cambodia in 2005, the authorities stated that while unusual, falling in love with a dog is not illegal. So Sarah Brown can relax.

Body Language
Swot up on body language and you can save yourself both time and money. We recommend Martin Lloyd-Elliott's excellent *The Secrets of Sexual Body Language.*

And in the Recession? Always remember: crossed legs = expensive, spread legs = cheap.

Bondage
Bondage tape, rope and silk scarves are all rather expensive when Poverty has her lash across your back. But revelling in physical bonds can really help take your mind off how badly your financial bonds are faring.

And in the Recession? Bag yourself a magician. They generally come with magician's rope as standard. It is the best bondage rope around and magicians are generally sad bastards and grateful for a shag.

Brothel
Sadly, in recessionary terms, perhaps something of a luxury we can no longer afford. Unless we're working as staff...

IS FOR

Communism

All for one and one for all etc., etc., etc.. "From each according to his ability to each according to his needs" actually sounds like a recipe for a lot of fun.

But consider this extract from Dr Zalkland's *The Revolution and Youth* – the 1925 publication which set down the guidelines for Correct Sexual Behaviour in the USSR.

1. The sexual act should not take place too often.

2. One should not change partners frequently.

3. Love should always be monogamous.

4. During the sexual act one should always beware of the possibility that a child may be conceived.

5. Sexual choice ought to operate according to class criteria and ought to conform to revolutionary and proletariat goals.

6. The class (ie The Party) has the right to intervene in the sex life of its members.

It was also stressed that 'sexual attraction for someone belonging to a different, hostile and morally alien class is a perversion of the same order as sexual attraction towards a crocodile or an orang-utan'.

And in the Recession? Remember this, Comrades, and think… things could be *so much worse*…

Corporal Punishment

The English Vice, they say. And also a great source of pleasure for many. Spanking and whipping, crops and paddles, the thwack of the Lochgelly Tawse across trembling buttock and the resultant blush of pink… like a sunrise on a much, much better day than any we have had lately.

And in the Recession? One of the few opportunities for a win/win situation left to us: simply power up a strong (and free) right hand and take out all your frustrations and disappointments upon the wobbling posterior of one of the ex-Public-Schoolboys-made-Partner in one of the many broken Banks around.

You will feel better, he will feel better (it's the only thing they know, poor loves) and you might even be able to charge him by the weal.

Cunnilingus

Also known as Dining at the Y, nibbling on the Hairy Clam or giving an Aussie Kiss (like a French Kiss, but 'down under') and altogether a marvellous pastime which will come into its own…

And in the Recession? If you are in a heterosexual relationship and are male then your partner will be so delighted that you have tried this without her resorting to blackmail or begging that she will be putty in your hands for weeks to come. Can't afford a Birthday/ Anniversary gift? Get behind those beef curtains and you are safe from criticism. If you are female, then… let's face it girls, you'd rather get head than a £2.99 Petrol Station bunch of flowers.

And anyone who just loves sashimi but finds Japanese restaurants just too pricey, now the pound is barely on the y of yen, can get the same enjoyment, completely calorie free, by going down on a girlfriend !

IS FOR

Detumescence
Something of a sexual metaphor for the Recession itself.

The coming down of what once was up. The softening of what once was hard.

Quite frankly it was boys running around with egoistical hard-ons and financial hard-ons that got us into this mess in the first place. And so a little detumescence might do us all no harm at all.

And in the Recession? Detumescence is the answer. For chaps, no hard on means none of the expenses associated with a hard-on: dinner, flowers, taxi, phone bill etc. And for girls? Let's face it, a night in with a friend who favours the flatter shoe, or even alone will almost certainly guarantee more in the way of orgasm than being plied with cheap wine by a boy in charge of a hard on he doesn't really know how to get the most out of.

What right do we have to rise until the pound does anyway?

The Right Reverend Rory McRoary writes: Man was created flaccid and flaccid should he remain except for reasons of procreational intimacy, for which the Church allows three hours each year (not to be taken together !). Pleasures of the flesh – anybody's flesh – are sinful and must be avoided through prayer, hymn singing or living in Aberdeen.

Dogging

Sadly what might have been a nice little earner has long been given away as a freebie.

And in the Recession? a) for the voyeurs, as a substitute for a night at the cinema or as a way of avoiding the outrageous costs of buying or downloading hardcore or b) for the participants, a way of passing off adultery (see infra) etc. as a form of performance art. NB: try dogging with a YBA (Young British Artist) and your cum-encrusted back seat might get the Turner Prize (£££££££!). Dog with Tracey Emin (hard to tell which one is which, isn't it?) and Tate Modern will have a tow truck with you by the time the last tissue has been tucked in the upholstery.

Dolls

Any of you who were around when Katie Price still had her own breasts will remember that 'Dolls' once meant pills... uppers, downers, trippers and the whole pharmacy. Feign the right problem and they can still be yours on the NHS, so get online and check your symptoms.

Alternatively you can go for the other kind of doll... given that the 'Living Doll' might be out of your price range at the moment, a few quid and a good pair of lungs can get you a girlfriend who never has a headache. Try any decent website and you can have a girl who looks like Jenna Jameson for just over twenty quid! Now that's what I call a saving.

And in the Recession? According to certain adventurous friends of mine there is a lot of fun to be had with Barbie that Mattel never foresaw.

Find a niece, borrow the Barbie and remember to hold on to her hair as she goes in... or you can lose her. Quick rinse under the hot tap and your sister's youngest will never know how much joy she has brought into the life of her favourite uncle/aunt.

Sexpert Andrea Gherkin says: A great opportunity to use this plastic symbol of man's enduring abuse and humiliation of woman in a suitable way. Stick this piece of plastic pornography where it belongs, sisters. In the shit. But don't let your boyfriend do it. That would be rape. In fact you shouldn't have a boyfriend. He's a rapist.

IS FOR

Enema

An acquired taste… well, not exactly taste. Let's say minority sport.

And in the Recession? For anyone who loves the old cover-you-in-custard sex or the oil-you-up and slip'n'slide stuff, the use of an enema could provide you both with a lubricating substance which is not only free, but totally organic and from a sustainable source. A great boon to those who are cash strapped but with an ecological conscience.

Exhibitionism

If you've got it, flaunt it, they do say. And for some this is a great turn-on. More stylish than dogging, more creative than flashing.

And in the Recession? Remember how you used to flaunt your car? Your house? Your Rolex Platinum Oyster which tells the time on Mars, is bullet-proof and has a Valet Parking function? Well, now you have none of these left to your name, you can still flaunt the great, hot, non-stop, acrobatic, tantric sex life you are enjoying. Even if you are not. The important thing is that everyone is still envious of you. Not that they actually have anything to be envious about. Just enjoy a little face chewing and footling whenever anyone is looking, practice a few sound effects and a couple of quasi-orgasmic facial expressions and you will be the envy of everyone. Works equally well for male and female. Although female friends are more likely to point out the thin line between exhibitionism and 'making an exhibition of yourself'.

IS FOR

Fellatio

Also known as The Blowjob, A Solo on the Pink Oboe, Smoking the Beef and Putting Lipstick on the Dipstick. Men generally love giving a lady a Pearl Necklace, but, sadly, too many girls think it's icky. And just as many do it badly. It is a testament to the fortitude of the priapic male that they keep risking their all between the teeth of women who grit them at the mere mention of cock-sucking. Skull-fucking (as a dear friend of mine wittily refers to it) has, over the years, spawned one of Life's Three Great Lies: "I promise I won't cum in your mouth". Sadly for men, your being Recession-struck is probably going to take that Holy Grail of a girl, the Titanic, even further out of your reach. What is a Titanic? Why, someone who goes down on her first time out.

And in the Recession? It is a sucker's market more than ever. I am reminded of the little girl who caught her mother on her knees giving Daddy head. "Is that what you do when you want to get babies?" she squeaked. "No sweetheart, that's what you do when you want to get jewellery" replied Mummy.

Feminist
(Ms Gherkin was asked to comment on the original entry here, but she stated, "This whole thing shrieks

Sexism. I will rewrite it with the open-minded fairness only a women can bring to the page." Ed)

Andrea Gherkin writes: When God made man she was obviously premenstrual and, since then, throughout herstory, we women have been degraded and abused by them. Who was responsible for the Great Flood? The Extinction of The Dinosaurs? The Fall of the House of Usher? Men! Who Let The Dogs Out? Men!

Sisters, you must reclaim your Inner Goddess, embrace your vagina (there are punani yoga excecises to help with the necessary flexibility in my new book *Men Are Bad, Throw Stones At Them*) and unleash together a tsunami of oestrogen across the world.

And in The Recession? The one thing that is still going up while everything else goes down, sisters, is the amount of money a real feminist can trouser by simply getting a job in a predominantly male environment, wearing low cut tops and then suing for £2 million for sexual harassment if anyone notices. And don't forget, should you fancy a paid holiday in these troubled times then get a highly paid job you really can't handle, get pregnant before anyone notices and then, voila, maternity leave ! And once the thing arrives, sell it to some broody anorexic actress. That's GirlPower

!

Flagellation

The thwack of leather on skin, the crack of birch on shoulder... a blessing both to he who gives and he who receives. Or she, of course. There are few sexual kinks that can be traced right back to the person that the social commentator, William Connolly, dubbed 'The Man in the Jaggy Bunnet'.

But flagellation can. From Golgotha to Max Mosely, it has remained one of the most popular pastimes for perverts everywhere.

And from earliest times, no matter how tight-arsed they might be about any other form of enjoyment, even the most religious types couldn't resist handing out or recieving a bit of a scourging. To this very day, many Holy Orders still indulge. The literal translation of Opus Dei is, in fact, "Lash for the Lord". Flagellation is generally accepted as established religion's clever alternative to masturbation. And long may they continue to enjoy it.

And in the Recession? Flagellation can almost become a full time job! Droves of devastated City Boys and Bankers who know no other way to atone, who regress, as you watch, to become snivelling Fortescue Minor whose fagging has failed to come up to scratch, or whose Latin Prep contains more gross errors than RBS's accounts are everywhere, looking for a strong right arm. And they must be soundly beaten. Expect to earn £100 a session. DO NOT take cheques or credit cards!

Frottage

Now don't grimace, we have all been there. Remember those teenage bump and grind sessions? Only a few buttons undone here and there, allowing for some attempted Etch-a-Sketch* action and plenty fully-clad crotch to crotch contact. That is frottage, my friends. Don't knock it.

And in the Recession? Frottage is freely to be found everywhere. You can double your Recession-beating tactics by leaving the car in the garage and getting a bike. Cheap commuting and perfect for a little added enjoyment en route to and from work. Should you live in Edinburgh, York or any other city where there are still plenty cobbled streets you are really in luck. If you are a public transport sardine, travel at peak times and frottage is pretty much unavoidable. And, it has to be said, not always pleasurable. Finding yourself in contact at all points with some BUFFY* who looks like she has Don King in a headlock* could put you off this enjoyable pastime for good.

*Etch-a-Sketch: the practice of trying to get a smile on a young lady's face by twiddling both nipples at the same time

*BUFFY: Big Ugly Fat Fucking Yeti. A young lady with a 'really great personality'

*Having Don King in a Headlock: having an exuberance of underarm hair.

IS FOR

GBL

Ecstasy. That stuff is just soooo '90s. Like, when we had money and shit. 50p a pop gets you a hit of the new party rider, GBL. Buy it now off the Internet while it's still legal!

And in the Recession? Also doubles as a date rape drug, for those of you who wish to shag beyond your impoverished means.

G-Spot

Time is money as they say, so ladies, don't waste another second on a man who needs patience and understanding while he 'explores' your pleasure regions.

And in the Recession? From now on, make it your prerogative to only date cartographers or gynaecologists.

Group Sex

The perfect synesthesic vehicle. A banquet of flesh might just help take your mind off your rumbling stomach, now that dinner is one potato and half a carrot between six of you.

And in the Recession? Afterwards, you can all cuddle up like a litter of puppies and save on the heating bill.

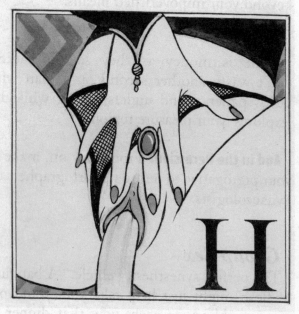

IS FOR

Humilitation

Let's face it. If all you're now living off is your memories of driving that red hot Ferrari to your sterling cold Canary Wharf office every morning, you're probably feeling humiliated enough.

And in the Recession? Only for the hardened masochist: walk up to the till at Harrods with a large leather handbag, call up your automated telephone banking service, and put your mobile on loud speaker just as the hollow voice politely informs you just how many minus pounds you have in your bank account. At this point, the sales assistant may well try to offer some sage economic advice. "There's a Primark on Oxford Street, you know, Sir…"

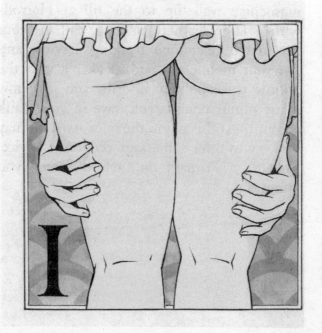

IS FOR

Impotence

Gentlemen, you may find erectile dysfunction is a side effect of losing your job and place in society. But don't worry; being an unemployed Countdown viewer who can't get it up when

Carol Vorderman's hot young mathematical replacement crunches her numbers *doesn't* mean you're not a man.

And in the Recession? Still out for the count down there? You'll save on condoms/shoes/a new kitchen, especially once your girlfriend/wife/lover leaves you for a 'working' man.

Incest

Sexual encounter between two or more members of the same immediate family. If conception occurs, possible side effects in resultant offspring may include club foot, hair lip and Type II diabetes, thus enabling you to claim disability support and boost your weekly income.

And in the Recession? Christmas shopping can be so expensive. How about 2 for 1s? If you're a boy, combine your mother and girlfriend (father and boyfriend if you're a girl) and one present will satisfy both, leaving you more money to put into your future childrens' 'they fuck you up' therapy fund.

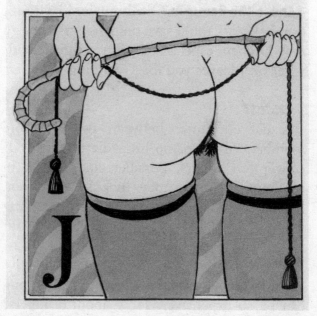

IS FOR

Jung

Not as sexy as old Sigmund but then Jungian analysts aren't quite as bad as the Freudian lot, less anally obsessed but then more airy-fairy and will quite likely ask you some very silly questions about your dreams. And if your analyst puts his hand up your skirt/down your trousers at roughly the same time as you think that he/she might do just that, you can both put it down to synchronicity and congratulate yourselves.

And in the Recession? Invoking Jungian archetypes is cheaper than taking hallucinogenic drugs to access your alter ego.

Prof Schnurr says "I remember meeting Professor Jung in the 1950s. I went to see him in his lovely house by the lake in Zurich. He was already quite old and we sat in the conservatory. He smoked his pipe. It smelt awful and I thought about my ex-wife, Frau Prof. Albertine Schnurr. His English housekeeper brought us tea. She was stark naked, but Carl Gustav reassured me by suggesting that this was an extreme case of transference, although he could not rule out syncronicity between the shag he was smoking, Albertine and the naked housekeeper. After she left, we ate Linzer Torte and talked about death. Just then one of his four secretaries came in to announce that my taxi had arrived. She was also naked. "Quite remarkable," said Jung.

IS FOR

Kegel Exercises

Come the credit crunch, it's time to do those Kegel Krunches. You'll feel ever so virtuous when your vagina can squeeze a man's cock hard enough to bring tears to his eyes or you can hit the ceiling with your seminal blast.

Kissing

Ah, kissing… remember the days before we needed a litre of Dom Perignon, 10gm of the white stuff and a bespoke Agent Provocateur feather duster to have a good time? No? Well, take my word for it, kissing was what we used to do for fun on the cheap. And now that you can't afford M&S Camembert, you'll taste so much more delicious in the morning.

And in the Recession? Take yourself off to the nearest children's playground, with a like-mouthed companion. Six-pack of White Lightning and a white Addidas pussy pelmet optional. (NB: Ensure selected playground is deserted before entering, or expect to find your mug-shot on the front of the *Daily Mail* in the morning).

IS FOR

Lap Dancing

Beleagured bankers. At the moment they are sobbing into their redundant Corby trouser presses. But very soon they may be flooding job centres nationwide and agreeing to work for less than the Polish immigrants who harvest our cauliflowers (they aren't great with numbers, remember). Hell, they used to have business meetings in Spearmint Rhino, so they must have picked up a trick or two. It would be an easy redeployment, with little retraining cost to the taxpayer, if we just sent those men to work it down the greasy pole.

And in the Recession? If you're feeling particularly sadistic and/or require an extra grind, shout 'Bonus'. Monopoly money at the ready…

Leather

Leather is another one of those luxuries few of us can now afford. Since the glory days of materialistic consumption are over, why not go the whole hippy hog and forgo the squeezing of one sorry hide into another by proclaiming yourself a 'real' vegetarian. Some people will respect you. Many will know exactly what you are up to.

And in the Recession? Coats, shoes and gloves and gimp masks you purchased before you lost your job can still be modelled on a

"The poor critters would have been sacrificed fruitlessly otherwise" basis. We suggest you tipex this on to all said items before dressing. It will save you the trouble of having to carry a portable audio device on repeat proclaiming your ethical credentials when you wear any of the aforementioned garments.

Lubricant

Let's face it. Lubricants that don't perish rubber or give you a case of internal hives are pretty much all alike. Similar to baked beans, it's the packaging you pay for, not the substance, which is generally made up to an identical recipe, albeit with a different E-numbered, fruit-salad scent. And with so many storecupboard staples for the pillaging, I suggest you forgo the Astroglide and make your way down the condiment aisle of your local Morrisons.

And in the Recession? Olive oil – extra virgin if you have a cheap sense of irony. But let's face it, who can afford olive oil anymore? Lard is thriftier but could be mistaken for thrush, so you could always try a fair drizzling of saliva, combined with a squirt of some own-brand household cleaner. The former is free, the latter cheaper than tiger balm, and less lurid than tabasco, plus the chemical cocktail is bound to kill any potential STDs. And potentially your ability to reproduce, ergo bringing us back to contraception...

IS FOR

Marriage

If you're a girl, don't think of yourself as a failure if you're not in this particular club. Married sex is cheap, yes, but the variety's crap, and don't ever forget: as a single girl, you were actually getting *rewarded* for sex.

And in the Recession? Married men, consider youselves lucky. Very.

Massage

Massage parlours are pricey and the nearest thing this country has to brothels. But a) they usually only supply 'relief massage' (yuk! How impoverished is that?) and b) they're only for men, although start up an exclusive, girls-only massage and sauna place staffed by hunky males and you might be on to a winner.

And in the Recession? Buy yourself a book. We recommend Gordon Inkeles' *Sensual Massage Made Simple*. It's much cheaper to get your date/partner/spouse to rub Flora into all those exciting nooks and crannies.

Mistress

See also: *Adultery*. Mistresses aren't always as dumb as is often suggested. They avoid marriage (qv), after all. In hard times mistresses are fine and dandy as long as they aren't so much *poules de luxe* as German Industrial Heiresses. But were that the case you wouldn't be lavishing diamond-studded Cartier watches upon them at the same time as telling your wife to cut down on the washing powder. She would be spoiling you.

And in the Recession? If you're really determined, you could try a time-share mistress.

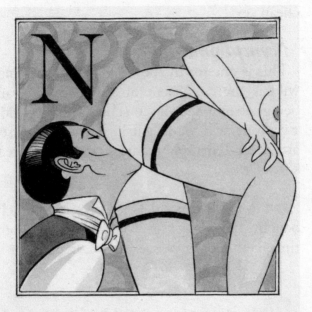

IS FOR

Nocturnal Emissions

The only trouble with wet dreams is that you often wake up after the event. And if you're fastidious, you have to deal with the, uh, soiled sheets.

And in the Recession? Definitely cheaper than masturbation. And it just proves that you've opted for total abstinence, the *ne plus ultra* of cheap sex.

Nymphomania

This is one for the boys. A nymph running wild is the equivalent of an ice cream van being abandoned in a school playground. Everyone will want a lick. Men, of course, are natural nymphomaniacs, in an inverted sort of way.

And in the Recession? For girls? Not much benefit. This sort of sex would be free in boom times, too. For boys, see Body Language…

IS FOR

Orgasms

How do you make your orgasms cost-effective? This is, admittedly, a tough one. For starters, look at the mind-boggling variety. There are fake orgasms, clitoral orgasms, anal orgasms, simultaneous orgasms and, where Mark Hix is concerned, food orgasms. Stephen Bayley could, without a shred of doubt, tell you all you need to know about an automotive orgasm, by which we mean the car variety. Proust came close to a memory orgasm with his madeleines.

And in the Recession?? We think the faked orgasm is the most expedient. They cost nothing in time or effort and whilst most convincingly performed by a female thespian, even men can get away with this, claiming dehydration if challenged for absence of material evidence.

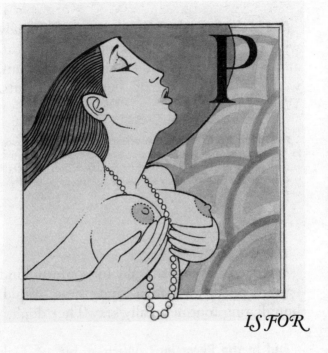

IS FOR

Pheromones

Some people call them BO and recommend a course of Lifebuoy soap or a decent deodorant. Others hail pheromones as the future of synthetic sexual attraction. Tests have proved that women will be more inclined to sit down in a cinema seat sprayed with male pheromones than the unsprayed, adjacent seats.

And in the Recession? Spray yourself liberally with pheromones, or work up a good sweat, and, in the darkness of a cinema auditorium, wedge your head, face up, between two seats. Wait patiently.

Prof Schnurr says "In my native town of Braunau in Austria, it is the custom for the women to rub their vulva with their handkerchief and give it to their lovers while they dance the polka to wipe the perspiration from their faces. It is without doubt a double pheromone strategy and, in my experience, a highly successful one.

Pole Dancing

Women have been told by some unkind bastard/bitch that men find these stupid, humiliating routines really sexy. They don't.

And in the Recession? With a bit of luck it will die out entirely as men will want to spend their precious squondoolacs on something more palpably rewarding than ogling a woman emulating a tethered Russian gymnast gyrating to the strains of Abba, however fit she may be.

Polyandry

Should not be confused with the left-wing journalist of a vaguely similar name. Come the next sexual revolution, when women take over the world and run the global banking system in order to prevent a similar Recession ever reoccurring, they will doubtless institute a culture of multiple husbands, as possession of several will demonstrate incontrovertible evidence of their wealth and status.

And in the Recession?? Watch out men, the petticoat millennium is coming…

Pornography

It's been around for 35,000 years, but should pornography exist? As a word, we mean? Shouldn't it be replaced by the acronym SAMs? Sexually Arousing Material(s)? It would remove all that stigma at one fell swoop. Obviously there's good and bad porn. Jacqui Smith will tell you about bad porn. Her husband will tell you about the good, Virgin-approved variety.

And in the Recession? Hard to know if the current amplitude of free Internet sex will continue. But currently it's your best bet by far. Seek out a cracking good broadband deal. Or *PornWeek*.

Priapism

No laughing matter if you have a hard-on that is permanent because it usually means you've got a life-threatening disease of the spine or your blood. Unless you live in the Kalahari desert. Even a Pfizer-induced erection that threatens to break all records will eventually go down, like Royal Bank of Scotland shares.

And in the Recession? Always look on the bright side of life, as the ditty goes. If you're too ugly to be a porn movie success (and you would be), you can be the life and soul of the party as a living-statue-cum-hat-stand.

Prof Schnurr says "In my field trip to the Kalahari with my wife and esteemed colleague, Frau Professor Elfriede Schnurr, I was able to observe the Priapismus at first hand. The tiny bushmen of that region come across a potential mate so rarely that they are in a permanent state of reproductive readiness. Elfriede was accorded the rare honour of an exclusive invitation to the Ceremony of the Stones, never before witnessed by a Westerner. She found it exhausting, but later told me that it had been a true vocational reward.

Shirley Balls says "Wow! Fab! Bring those hard'n horny old Bush men on! I think those Republican guys are sooooo fit! They sure rack up my raunch-rating!!

Prostate Gland

The Male G-spot is located, most unfortunately, up the male poop-chute. This is where divine sensations are produced when you slip a lubricated finger up his bum, locate the walnut-shaped gland and gently rub.

And in the Recession? You mean you haven't worked it out? Use prostate gland massage as a form of currency. Although remember, some men will leap six feet in the air if you even touch their tush.

Shirley Balls says "C'mon gals! Go get those Marigolds! Sometimes you just gotta hold your nose and dive in there to take your fellah to heaven! Refusing to stick a digit where a midget fears to tread just isn't playing the game.

IS FOR

Queening

Is when a woman sits naked on her partner's face. Some men love this because they are in a position to access and appreciate (at extremely close quarters) all the seldom seen parts of her anatomy and pay them homage, or more likely, lip service. Handcuffs and restraints can add to the feelings of utter inadequacy in the presence of such awesomely presented organs. Not to be confused with the activities of the late, much-mourned, Quentin Crisp.

And in the Recession? You could turn this into an expression of female domination and insist that he pays you for the privilege of jamming his nose up your spam fritter. But careful there... too much of this malarkey and he might just ask you to reciprocate. Queen for a day and then move on, we would advocate.

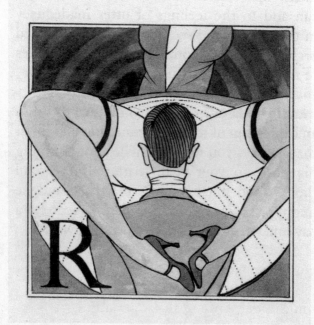

IS FOR

Rough Trade

A sexual partner of the working class whose lover has middle or upper class pretensions. There are some women and male gays who find it particularly thrilling to have torrid sex with 'crude, dirty, rugged males'. Connie Chatterley and Mellors probably started the rot.

And in the Recession? Now that we live in a classless society (thanks to John Major's 1990's speech), you'll only be able to prove your crude/dirty/rugged credentials by speaking like Phil Mitchell in *East Enders*, and slapping her around a bit. But it's a lot of work for little reward.

Rubber

Boys love rubber more than girls, unless you're talking a £600 corset outfit from House of Harlot. We think it's something to do with motor racing. Or watching motor racing in the rain wearing a smelly wet rubber mac. As you can tell, I'm not really an enthusiast.

And in the Recession?

I hear rubber ground sheets are very good value. Second hand, they should only cost about £25.

IS FOR

Speed dating

I always thought this meant that the date was over in a flash and the dater didn't have to go to bed with the datee. But no, now I know better. You all meet in a large room and the girls sit at small tables and the guys come and sit down and have a minute or so to talk about themselves and how wonderful they really are even thought they look exactly like a Four. Then, just as you think you're getting somewhere, she opens her mouth…

And in the Recession? Speed dating is not only a growth industry, but one that is proving, just like Internet dating, particularly popular in this Recession. The reasons for a dating surge of 40% among women alone (in the US, where the effects of the Recession have been felt earlier) is because unemployed or underemployed people have more time to surf the Web and online dating is a relatively inexpensive way to date people. And offline dating events are cheaper than a series of disastrous blind dates. People appreciate the comfort of another human being and in difficult and uncertain times, love is more important than ever before.

IS FOR

Testicles

Having balls is really important in a Recession – whichever sex you are. You've got to seize each day by the scruff of the neck and wrestle it like a tiger. Or, in Ruth Padel's case, a leopard, or a Nobel prize-winning West Indian poet.

Technique

We all tend to forget that this can change you from a Four to a Two. Caveman/woman sex is fine for five minutes, but then you've got to refine your act. Read Susan Quilliam's excellent *The New Joy of Sex*, or (just to show we have no favourites around here) Suzi Godson's *The Sex Book*. Either or both of these excellent tomes will give you a refresher/renewed-awareness course. If sexual technique is the only thing you have to offer, you'd better be damned good at it.

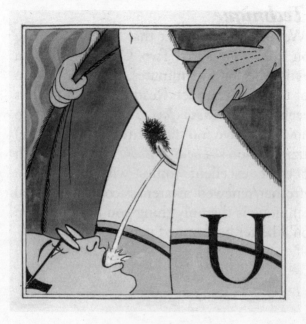

IS FOR

Urolagnia

Nothing to do with a delay in converting euros into pounds, more to do with peeing. From Rembrandt to Havelock Ellis, blokes have been entranced by the Golden Shower. Urolagnia comes in two sizes: a) watching someone pee or being watched while peeing. and b) peeing on someone or being peed on by someone.

And in the Recession? Watersports are perfect for a recession – as we've already pointed out elsewhere in this book – for their ecological and economical properties. With trusted partners, i.e., ones who you've already shared body fluids with for some time, pee is sterile, and you can have a lot of, er, creative fun.

If you drink your own pee, it's apparently jolly good for you and anti-ageing. J.D. Salinger drank his. Sarah Miles drinks hers, although she never offered me any. You can mix it with fruit juice if you don't like the taste.

Urolagnian tip: Don't try imbibing your pee unless you're a veggie. Meat eaters' pee contains too much urea, which is potentially harmful.

Voyeurism

This is where you derive sexual pleasure from watching others having sex. There are two sorts of voyeur, the open voyeur and the clandestine voyeur. Exhibitionists and voyeurs should team up in the Recession. It's only fair…

And in the Recession? Come to *Mama!* The Recession was practically *invented* with this in mind. It's cheap (indeed, for the opportunist, free) no more than the price of a return ticket to the hideout of your choice and some thermal underwear. Try not to get caught by the local Neighbourhood Watch vigilante group. Lynching can be nasty.

Vulvic

Often confused with a brand of mineral water. Actually means 'pertaining to the vulva'. We've only included it here because we think it's a strange and splendid word. Almost as good as the pulp-porn-fiction 'cuntal'.

IS FOR

Writing Erotica

Contrary to popular view, this is not as easy as you might think. But at least it doesn't earn you a lengthy term in the slammer these days.

Would-be erotic authors often approach us with their short stories or their four hundred-page epic erotic novel. Many think they are called, but very few are chosen.

Sex is very difficult to write both seriously and well. You're better off trying to be funny. But, a bit like patting your head and rubbing your tummy at the same time, being turned on and laughing are totally inimical to each other.

And in the Recession? Nothing ventured, nothing gained. Who knows, you might be the next Belle de Jour. Publishers, we're told, in their knee-jerk, Pavlovian way, are looking for something 'naughty but nice' to fill Belle's elegant high heels just now.

Shirley Balls says "I just LOVE erotica. One day I'm going to write a best-selling novel. Can't be that hard. Me and Kent like to go to bed with a really good book like Lesbian Warriors From Outer Space or Nympho Secretaries and their Toy Boys. I get down to reading while he goes down on me. It gives me loads of inspiration for my Sexpert books!"

IS FOR

XXX

Which used to denote a really hot porn movie or sex act. Both of which are now so commonplace as to have made 'XXX' more associated with indifferent Aussie lager. Or was that four X's?

And in the Recession? Who cares – indifferent lager is all you'll be drinking these days.

X Position

Which goes something like this: Man lies down on back and Woman lowers herself on to his erect member, facing him. He then sits up while she leans back, forming an X shape, sort of. The sex should be slow and languorous so that they can enjoy looking at each other's bodies. So make sure you're a Four looking at a Two.

And in the Recession? We're not sure what the recessionary value of this is but hey, there just aren't that many things that begin with X.

Yoni

The Hindu opposite of your lingam. However 'you silly yoni' has not really caught on in this country, despite our sizeable Hindi-speaking population.

Youth

"Sex is wasted on the Young," someone once said, but I think it's more a case of Youth is wasted on Youth.

And in the Recession? As most teenagers are too busy making themselves into paranoid schizophrenics on skunk to enjoy sex in all its full glory, they would do better taking up with a Sugar Daddy or Mummy who could introduce them to some more grown-up drugs like Sevruga, uncut Columbian Marching Powder or Chateau Petrus. These are more conducive to a better grade of rumpy-pumpy.

IS FOR

Zoophilia

Like Bestiality only not so selective. Popular among animal rights activists, although usually ends badly when they try miscgeny in the local zoo's lion house. Still, proves Darwin right, cuts down on social services, and shortens the Recession. Win-win.